SHARKS & BUTTERFLIES

John D Robinson

Cover art by Janne Karlsson.

Printed in the U.S.A.
Published by **Cajun Mutt Press**

I dedicate this book to **C**armelina, **B**onita, **G**race, **A**va, **S**tanley.

Thankful acknowledgements are given to the hard working Editors and Publishers where some of these poems first appeared:

Underground **B**ooks, **Z**ombie **L**ogic **R**eview, **B**old **M**onkey, **D**ead **S**nakes, **H**orror **S**leaze **T**rash, **C**avalcade **O**f **S**tars, **M**ad **S**wirl, **T**he **C**hicago **R**ecord.

Contents:

[...]

THE SEDUCTION

I've seduced the webs of spiders and
danced with the final breath of a
broken summer: I've been drunk
and read my poetry in a church,
I've looked for something, never
knowing what it was, I may have
found it and lost it without being
aware:
I've exhibited and sold some
of my paintings,
I've had books of my poetry
published, I've prowled the
scenes as an outsider, been
described as an outlaw,
I've drowned in shapes of
reclusive whispers and
hiked the trail of
migrating embers of a wasted
life and find myself here
amongst the laughing
ashes of a tip-toeing
breeze whose birth
certificate,
expired some time ago.

A CORRECTION OF BIBLICAL PROPORTIONS

Let's talk it straight,
Jesus was known to take wine
what is not so commonly known
was that He
was also a pot-head,
fine and beautiful
middle east grass
the most spiritual of all weed
God's own personal stash!
One day 5000 people follow Jesus to a place
that was sparse and dry and isolated;
they wanted to hear his words and
they wanted to see something impressive.
First thing that Jesus did
was to turn the masses on with some Heavenly weed
and to calm things down a little and to help prepare
the peoples for a teaching;
During His sharing of Love and Wisdom, the masses became hungry; they got the munchies as a result of the sacred weed; they became a little restless as their stomachs rumbled and groaned.
Jesus had a situation he hadn't expected;
before Him were 5000 hungry, potential believers and he
needed to help them out or his reputation would be shot,
oh shit!
A couple of his disciples
managed to scrounge up two fish
and five loaves of bread
and then,
hey man
a miracle
'The feeding of the 5000'
Initially

It was
‘The weeding of the 5000’
but history and time
and words and politics
have altered and distorted
such learning.

A GUY CALLED HENRY THAT YOU DIDN'T KNOW

"**G**ive me a kiss!" he said.
"Listen Henry," I said smiling,
"I've a reputation to upkeep
and kissing a drunken gypsy
in a hotel room on a Friday
afternoon could rip it apart;
besides what would my seniors
at the office think!
HEY! What the fuck
would my wife say?"
"GO ON! GIVE ME A KISS!"
he roared, swaying on his feet,
beer can in hand,
grinning a black-toothed,
gold-toothed grin.
"It's out of the question Henry," I said
and then, "Here, I've brought
you some food"
"YOU DO LOVE ME!"
Henry barked, laughing.
I nodded slowly; I couldn't deny it;
Henry was Roma,
he was a scoundrel
and a husband and father,
a brother and an uncle
and grandfather,
he was a drinker and a gambler
and a friend and enemy to many
and he was one of the most endearing
and honest of people I have ever met;
he made me laugh and smile
and he provoked me into thinking

and contemplating like few people
have done and he lived life as it came at him.
Dead now; perhaps four or five years;
heart attack;
Henry was prepared for his end,
the world didn't stop,
not even for a moment
and he wouldn't have wanted it to.

THE WOODEN DECKING

Stumbling, it came across the
wooden decking; a wasp-like
insect, it's right wings missing
and every now and then it would
flip over onto its back, its legs
frantically kicking at the
crushing air and suddenly it
righted itself and then hobbled
forward and then back-tracked
and then flipped over onto
it's back and again kicked its legs
furiously and then it lurched
forward and then it
suddenly stopped moving.
I watched and waited and
the sun was warm and the
neighbours were out and I waited
and thought of alcohol
and of love and of survival and
I looked back down at the now
lifeless thing, still and calm and
dreamless and I thought of
my grandchildren and of the shitty
day that I'd had
but at least it hadn't ended up
breathless upon the wooden
decking and at 5 p.m. on another
forgettable day, I feel thankful
that my heartbeats, that I
can feel the pushing of an April
breeze and hear small nature rustling
in its path

and I look down once more at
the dead insect; now a convenience
food for a spider
and soon
I will no longer be alone and soon
I will talk and listen to a
loved one, soon, the death of
this insect will be forgotten
and the hours will continue to
make dust of us all and soon we
shall no longer hold hands or
hear the wind-chimes calling from
our infancy.

IN RECENT YEARS

It was his 43rd birthday and we celebrated
by drinking,
we drank a lot together
and in recent years he'd been in and out
of prison and had remarried
and
we were getting to know each other
a little and every now and then we
punched one another;
some kind of
macho thing between us I guess,
his wife was a spiteful pill-head;
we returned to his apartment,
we were
drunk,
his wife was laying naked,
passed-out on a bed,
we drank the last of the take-aways
whilst we listened to
Johnny Cash
then I left to meet
a girl and go to a
party.
I never saw him alive again and
we were getting to know each other.
'Death by misadventure ' the
Coroner decided
by way of alcohol
and prescription drugs;
he died on his birthday
aged 43
and he was my dad.

JULIAN

Julian was tall and skinny,
too skinny maybe and he
was gentle, articulate, creative
and very effeminate in
his mannerisms and
manners;
when we first met
he was kicking heroin
and for 3 or 4 days
I witnessed his
withdrawal and I held
him and he clung to me
and then he found
God and fell in love
with a friend of mine
who had also recently
been re-born;
they married and
had 2 sons, the marriage
lasted perhaps
several years and
then Julian split with
God and his wife and
children and
found a male lover
and moved from town
to city; his sons
visited a few times
and returned with
tears and cigarette
burns and bad dreams
and they never saw

their father alive
again and neither
did I.
Later, his lover
died of HIV AIDS
and Julian had
same diagnosis and
he committed
suicide
and I remember Julian
one time telling me
of blowing truck drivers
in midnight deserted
car parks and that
he would have
done anything for
a needle-push of
heroin but God had
saved him;
there's a lot more
to this story
as there will be
to yours,
but for now,
for Julian,
this will do it.

THE SCRIPT

Her name was Clare, she was a few
years older than my I;
Clare had big breasts that
mesmerised me and she
would flirt with me, move in
real close and make me blush
and turn away –
"Would you do something
for me?" Clare asked
of me one day, "I'd really
appreciate it" she said
smiling and thrusting out
her chest.
"Okay" I said.
"Would you go and cash
this script?" she said
handing me a prescription
that was tightly folded
into a small square;
as I took the paper from
her hand, her fingers
softly and briefly clasped
mine and she fluttered
her eyes and I looked
at her wonderful
cleavage and said
"Sure, okay"
The pharmacy was
close by, on the way
I unfolded the script,
a blind man could have
seen the obvious added

forgery
for amphetamine;
that didn’t stop me,
I thought of Clare’s
breasts and that
beautiful cleavage.
“It’ll take a few
minutes to process,
please take a seat”
said the pharmacist
smiling and friendly.
I sat down and just
a few minutes later 2
plain-clothed police
officers, a male and
female, approached me
and placed the hand of the
law upon me and took me
down to the station
where I was finger-printed,
questioned, to which I
responded with silence
and then placed into a
cell –
40 minutes later I
heard the wailing and
confessing, screeching
tearful tones of Clare;
On the day of our
court appearance Clare
wouldn’t even look
at me and her mother
believed that I had
forged the script and

looked at me with
disgust;
we received 12 months
probation each.
Several years later I
learnt that Clare had been
involved in an RTA and
was now in a forever
wheelchair,
but
I could only think of
those breasts,
of that magical cleavage
as she dances
free and child-like in
an amphetamine whirl
of sensual
eternal ecstasy.

THE CABLE WIRE

The scent of your
pleasure across
my mouth
takes me back
to earlier days
and to times
when time was
something we took
for granted and
treated it like
something casual
and uninteresting
and now,
some years later,
the taste of
your passion
is as sweet
as ever
and now the
clock-hands
dare not move
but rather they
hesitate and linger
like 2 flight-weary
birds resting awhile
upon a gently
swaying cable-wire.

THE SUPERMARKET SCENE

As I entered the
supermarket I
needed to step
quickly backward
to make way for
a sprinting
and laughing
teenager
with a hand-basket
full of groceries
in one hand and
clutched beneath his
other arm
a small baby;
that was bobbling
around and laughing
and having a
good time,
following very close
behind was another
laughing, sprinting
young guy;
he didn't have a baby
but had a hand-basket
in each hand, full of
beer and groceries.
The fat security guard
waddled very slowly
towards the exit/entrance
and stepped out into
the street,
he lazily swung his head

left and right
and then shrugged his
sagging shoulders and
frowned and said to
no one
"They've got away"
and then he
wobbled back into
the store;
"I'll have to phone this
in and then write it up;
it's gonna take me
some time"
and then he ambled
out of sight
towards the back of
the store;
I stepped back in
and looked over at
a grinning cashier;
"Your security
Is tight" I said.
The cashier smiled
and then shaking
his head said,
"Yeah, tighter than
Mother Teresa"
Leaving the store
I thought of the
baby,
now a potential
felon, an accessory
to robbery;
running away

in fear of capture
before he could
even walk into the
arms of his poor
mama.

WHEN UNCLE VISITED

My little sister had to
give up her bedroom
and share mother's bed,
father slept it off down
stairs and I was left
alone in my box-room;
we were told he was
an uncle
but he was a hobo bum
drinker my drunken
father met and felt sorry
for and brought him
home for a couple
of days warm comfort;
within hours we were
smothered in flea bites;
mother and father
argued behind closed
doors, but uncle
stayed and he smelt
terrible and he was
filthy and he was old
and toothless and he
ate food noisily and
never spoke a word
to my sister and I;
uncle didn't say
goodbye, he just
disappeared after 3
days;
mother called in a
pest control company

and my sister returned
to her bedroom
and uncle was never
seen again;
father vanished on
a 4 day drunk and
then returned with the
usual remorse and
alcoholic tears and
promises; no more
visiting uncles.

NO EXPECTATIONS

I stayed at home;
the house phone didn't ring
and the mobile was
switched off;
no fucker knocked on
the door to tell me
where my life was
going wrong.
I took some codeine and
smoked some joints and
then took the dog for a
walk and didn't see a single
asshole to bother me;
I made lunch and
afterward took a nap
and no one was expecting
anything of me and they
didn't get anything and
I listened to the radio and
didn't give a shit about
anybody else and it felt
good like a day-off from
every fucking thing in
this life that we've made for
one another.

MOBILE PHONES WHILST PISSING

Standing at the urinal,
my dick in my right hand;
half-way through, my
mobile sounded; with my
left hand I fish inside my
leather jacket, jiggling
and wriggling this way
and that and finally
retrieve the thing and
then I thumb a pad
and say "Yeah?"
"Hi; are you okay?" she
asks;
"Well, I've got my hands
full at the moment" I say
"Where are you? I can hear
an echo" she says;
"I'm taking a piss in a
supermarket crapper" I say
I look down at my shoes
and noticed I'd splashed
them; I glance over
at the guy in the next
urinal and for some
reason I wink at him;
he frowns, quickly zips
up and disappears;
"Are you there?" she
asks "I need some
cigarettes"
"They're bad for you"
I say

"So are you," she says
I don't argue.
"Okay," I say and
terminating the call
I zip up, wash my
hands knowing that I
am more dangerous
than a pack of cigarettes
and I step back into
the supermarket feeling
invincible as I join
the queue with the
other nicotine addicts.

SUMMER DREAMS

40 years ago; about 13
years old; returning
home from a train
journey; it was summer
and it was hot and as
I walked the slope to the
exit I could see up ahead
a woman
and a toddler crouched
down picking blackberries;
as I passed she said 'Hello'
I turned to return the
greeting;
she was in her early 20's,
pretty with her brown hair
tied back in 2 pig-tails;
she was leaning forward,
her loose-fitting blouse
falling open and providing
me with a clear view of
her breasts
and I was instantly taken
prisoner, captivated,
transfixed and mesmerised
by the wonder before me;
she told me of how the
blackberries were this year
and how she was going to
make a blackberry pie and
her toddler gazed up at me
as I gazed down at his
mother's lovely breasts and

that moment is with me
now, like it happened
just a few moments ago
and ever since that holy
vision that burnt and buried
itself deep into my psyche;
nothing compares to the
sight of a perfect pair
of beautiful breasts.

PERHAPS, TOO MANY

There are days,
perhaps too many,
when for my own
safety and for
that of others,
that I stay in bed
or at best don't
leave the house;
but even this
is no guarantee,
like today,
I was sat at the
kitchen table
reading from my
1st edition copy of
Dan Fante's
'A gin-pissing-raw meat-
dual carburettor-V8-
son of a bitch from
Los Angeles'
when there came a
knock at the door;
I was expecting nobody;
I put down the book
and barked
"Who the Fuck!"
I opened the door
to 2 silver-haired
retired
well dressed persons;
one male
one female;

"Yeah," I said looking
at the 2 of them;
"I've some pamphlets
here" the guy said
holding up some
glossy paperwork;
"Asking WHO REALLY
RULES THE WORLD?"
I glared hard at the
guy; fixing his eyes and
said
"I do"
the silver-haired lady let
go a soft nervous laugh;
when I looked over,
she stopped and looked
silently down at her shoes;
"Is that all?" I asked
looking back at the
silver-haired guy;
he looked puzzled
frowned and said
"Yes"
I closed the door and
made some espresso
and watched the rain
beginning to fall outside
and then
anxiously waited for
the next asshole to
intrude upon my life.

JUST LIKE YOU

I've seen god
in puddles of rain
in the scribbles
of babies
in the smiles
of the lost,
in the dew
and the dust
and in the
footsteps of
the nameless
just like you
I know god
as you know
a new morning
as I know a
new morning
I've seen god
in garages and in
cafes and bars and
public toilets and
in the eyes of cats
and in the doorways
of sulking cathedrals,
like you
I know god in the
flight of soft things
and in the voices of
oceans and alcohol
and what we call
love;
trying to make it work

with something
somewhere;
always looking over
our shoulders for
something that we
don’t have words
for;
knowing it is there
all the time;
somehow,
a faith in
the mystery
of it all.

THAT MORNING; EVERY MORNING

One morning
when he was
6 years old
he woke up to
find his 4 year
old sister lying on
the floor beside
his bed;
she was still, cold,
dead
and he couldn't
wake her up and he
didn't understand;
he went to find his
other younger
3 years old sister
and he found her
in bed, she was
still, cold, dead
and he couldn't
wake her up and
he didn't understand
and he began to
scream for his mama
but she didn't come,
she wasn't there, he was
alone and he couldn't
understand and he began
to cry;
several hours later
the police found him
alone and crying and

not understanding why
he couldn't wake up
his little sisters and why
his mama wasn't
there to cuddle him
and later he
understood that his
mama had murdered
his sisters and that
she had been unwell
and had been taken
to a locked hospital
and he couldn't
understand why his
mama had killed his
sisters and spared him
and
40 years later he still
doesn't understand and
he lives his life and
he is humble, truthful
and a sensitive soul
and he lives his life
one
moment at a time
and what
scares
and
warms
him
simultaneously,
is waking up
not knowing what
awaits in the world

as he
opens
his
eyes.

A DRINK WITH THE OLD MAN

I had left her in bed
it was early morning
and we needed
a loaf of bread;
by chance or fate
or bad luck
we met
and he asked
"Do you fancy a drink?"
"Of course," I said
"Where?" he asked
"Your choice" I answered;
we ended up on a
ferry crossing the
channel to Belgium
and for three days
and nights we stayed
drunk and crazy and
slept a few hours in
a bus depot and we
staggered into carnivals
and danced with
nuns and kissed the
hands of fat barmaids
and then
3 days later
returned home,
weak and fragile and
vulnerable
but my lady was angry
very angry;
"You bastard! I've

been phoning hospitals
and police stations for
3 fucking days, I didn't
know if you were
dead or alive!"
she screamed
"You're a lousy
thoughtless beast
and you didn't even
bring back a fucking
loaf of bread!"

THE PAST AND THE CURIOUS

As a young man
I was never a great
success with the
girls;
it wasn't that I
lacked the urge or
the desire but
rather I always felt
awkward and ugly
and always ended
up saying
something
dumb and I was
always the first to
get crazy drunk
and
get into some kind
of hassle;
naturally, I had my
times with the girls
and enjoyed the
majesty of their
flesh and gentleness
and their special
ways that I'll
never understand
and my curiosity
hasn't diminished;
I love women
and at over half
a century-old I'm
a little more at

ease with feminine
beauty and their
natural sensuous
ghosts
within their eyes
and lips and hair and
the way of their
sunsets; the way of
their worlds and
the music they make;
forever captivated
and
enchanted by the
flames of heaven
and hell.

TELLING THE TRUTH

A Friday night and
I can remember it was
summer and a group
of 7 or 8 of us 16
and 17-year-olds
were going into town
to get drunk and leer
at the girls;
as Bernard stepped
outside to join us
his mother appeared
in the doorway and
said
"Where are you going
boy?"
"Into town to get
smashed with my
friends" her son
answered;
"Don't you lie to me
now, tell me, where
are you going?" she
asked again;
"Into town to get drunk"
Bernard repeated "with
my friends"
"Now boy," she said
sternly "don't fool me
around, tell me where
you're going or I'll
call for your father!"
"Okay ma," Bernard said,

"I'm going to the park
to sniff some glue and
then I'm going to
hang around outside
the women's toilets"
"Well, why didn't tell
me that in the first
place and make sure
you're
quiet when you get
back" she said
slamming the door
closed.

MAYBE I SHOULD HAVE SAID

That I held no respect for
the department and
considered his manager
to be a spineless asshole
and
maybe I should have said
that
I couldn't give a fuck
about the politics and
policies
and that
'feathers in caps'
means nothing to me
and it was
way too little
way too late
and that I was going
nowhere
and so was he;
and he looked at me
with a look
of a young
man in the pursuit
of ambition
and he was looking
at someone, maybe
for the first time,
who had never
believed and who
had given up on
all that fairy-tale
bullshit

a very long time ago
and he said to me
without humour
"We can sort this out"
"That'll be good"
I said with a smile;
and maybe,
I should have
said that.

SORRY IN ADVANCE

'**H**e doesn't belong here, he
shouldn't be here, he's a
vicious individual when
drunk and beats his wife in
front of their young
children, this is not the
first time, he shouldn't be
in a psychiatric hospital,
he should be
in detox, rehab or prison:
apparently, when he's sober
he is a gentle compassionate
hard-working devoted
family man: when he
drinks, he doesn't become
mentally unwell or psychotic
but just plain aggressive
and vile' the ward nurse
said and the 12 other
professionals nodded and
agreed he'd be discharged
within 24 hours: once again
his wife will forgive him
as he begs for mercy and
forgiveness and swears that
he'll never hurt her again
and of how sad and ashamed
he feels and that he loves
her and the children and
that they are his world and he
hates himself, that is until he
opens the next bottle.

THE HOUNDING

'You've burnt yourself out these
past 3 years, you've been non-
stop publishing books and
broadsides, as well as getting
your own work into print'
'A rising star of the underground
poetry scene' one editor
recently wrote:
'Legendary' wrote another:
'9 chapbooks and a full
collection, hundreds of your
poems online and in print,
give it a rest, for fuck's sake!'
she advised, maybe, she's
right, my wife and editor,
but fuck it,
keep moving forward,
keep hounding the fuckers
with the poetry,
snapping at their heels,
keep the flames high
and never weaken
and don't look back
I tell myself as I write
this gazing into a mystery
of an august night.

MOVING ON

It was hard to ignore each other,
we were neighbours, around the
same age, 13 or 14 and for a
brief exciting exploratory time
we were close and although
we didn't make love, we stopped
just short a number of times:
we moved on and she married
and divorced a policeman,
no children and she died of
cancer in her early 40's;
she was beautiful
and so are you
all life has the potential
of beauty and I know
the sense of peace,
the numbness of distance,
of life and death and I
remember her fondly
like the first smile of my
daughter or watching my
shadow chase the
sinking sun and never
quite catching it.

THE DRAGONFLIES

Never knew her parents and has no regrets;
'Fuck them' she'll tell you:
bounced and beaten in children's
care-homes until 16 when she hit
the streets and crafted a taste for
speed: early 50's now,
shot to pieces, skin, teeth, hair,
body and prettiness withered,
hanging on like a tired fog,
a permanent stutter steals her
words and makes verbalising
herself frustrating and she'll
shout and scream gibberish
in her anguish:
she has a son,
they are strangers,
we all are, she'll tell you
'You only think you know
someone, you don't, you don't
even know yourself'
and then she shuffled away
towards the soup-kitchen
muttering beneath her
breath something about
dragonflies.

THE HUFF

Coming home, leaving behind a
frail confused 70-year-old about
to become homeless,
a 30-year-old male swallowing
a razor blade,
a 40-year-old female
fatal overdosing
on a bad batch,
the closing of desperate
hospital wards,
I read some Huffstickler and
smoked a joint, swallowed
some pills and listened to
Mendelson and Huffstickler
holds true and familiar and
the starkness and always
the gentleness and his words
rebound in my mind,
words that remind you and
I who we are, of what we
see ourselves as
coming home to harmony
to Huffstickler
is a blessing
we should all have.

LIKE A NEW-BORN

Although only a year older than I,
he made me look like a teenager
beside him: lived with his mom
and dad all his life, never worked,
never loved a lover but he'd
drink a bottle of whisky a day
and not eat a morsel for 6 weeks
and then collapsing in seizures
and alcoholic convulsions: both
parents recently dying within
weeks of each other, an estranged
brother owned the house and
kicked his drunken ass out;
he's been dry for about 3 weeks
and I helped to get a roof over
his head, albeit, temporary:
57 years old and lost,
bewildered, alien to the feeling
of self-responsibility, of
having no one, alone,
completely, utterly, alone in
our world like a new-born.

THE JAIL-BREAK

He'd piss and shit his pants, he'd
vomit constantly, everywhere,
he'd fall and sustain cuts and
injuries to his head, arms and
legs, vodka black-outs:
countless times he woke up in
hospital: his sober brother was a
charity-aid-worker and he didn't
give a fuck about his sibling,
no one did, he didn't give a
fuck about himself:
I wasn't shocked when I was
told that he had been found
dead, choked own his vomit:
I didn't feel sad but relieved for
him in a way I'd never felt
before, he was free of the
wretchedness that had
imprisoned him and I knew
he was never going to
make a jail-break.

THE DROOP

'Wow! I'm sorry, I mean,
it's not you, it's me!' I said
pathetically, confused and
disappointed:
'Look, don't worry, it
happens, it's the alcohol'
she said kindly:
'I've been drunk for years
and I've been fucking for
years and this has never
happened!' I was
embarrassed and in
shock:
'Please, it's nothing, lets
wait until morning then
see what happens' she
suggested:
at 7 a.m. I was fully restored
and by 8 a.m. we had sexually
exhausted one another and
lay satisfied as others were
making their way to the
offices, factories, buses,
trains, building sites, shops
I said 'Would you like some
wine? I've got a bottle in the
fridge.'
'Wine is the most important
drink of the day' she
replied and I knew we
were making it good.

THE FLOW

Fuck the flow, I'm not content to
go with it,
fuck the fashion and the in-tune
attitudes,
I've never been attracted to
the swing and hip,
at least not for too long,
swim against the tide,
swing in the shadows.

SHARKS & BUTTERFLIES

We were talking about butterflies and
how some species migrate thousands
over miles annually, moving up to
speeds of 30mph and riding the
swirling thermals and forceful
winds:
'The power and intelligence of
these delicate creatures can be
comparable to that of the great
white shark' I said
he smiled widely and nodded his
head slowly: we were stoned on
potent hash and Valium,
our eyes mere slits,
our throats dry
our minds and bodies
saturated with a heavy
peacefulness that made
discussing the beauty and
wonder of butterflies and
sharks in the same breath as
something quite natural
as then, the silent t.v. screened
pictures of the
horrific aftermath of a
suicide bomber in the beating
heart of a food market
someplace in the world.

THE EVERYDAY DESIRE

Sex is a life-time everyday desire,
preoccupation, forever present, it
constantly plagues and thrives in
the imagination, we all crave it,
some viciously force it,
some pay for it,
some go solo
some abstain
some make a very healthy
monetary living from it
from in the streets
to in a studio
I've never given or made cash
from sex
I've known plenty who have,
those who have paid have generally
been creepy, socially isolated and
inept males of all ages,
those who sold sex have been both
male and female and mostly its
been cash for drugs or booze,
there doesn't seem to be much
fun in buying or selling sex,
it's a business like any other,
the oldest profession
but like all money-making
activities, the bosses are usually
unfeeling, unflinching, care-
fuck-all except for themselves
and pimps, I hear,
are no fucking different.

THE MUTTERED HYMNS

She jumped in her mid-teens from
middle-class university future into
the world of sex and drugs: speed
was her choice and later, alcohol:
our mothers were life-long friends
so she and I had known each
other since toddlers: I was sweet
on her and, I think she felt the
same but we never got it
together:
she had two daughters by
some fucking vicious speed-
freak, she couldn't look after
them and they were removed
from her care:
she became obliterated,
homeless, her body swelled
and her skin yellow and she
died a few weeks after a
savage beating from some
useless piece of shit:
a few years previous she
had called on me: we sat
and drank wine and smoked
hash, she wasn't in too bad shape,
I had thoughts of intimacy but I
knew she was vulnerable and
maybe lonely and looking for a
little safe friendship where she
could relax for a while and
that was enough:
she was cremated, a small

number attended: one of her
daughter's was serving 15
years for attempted murder
and was handcuffed to 2
prison officers, her other sister
was present, both were weeping:
prayers were said and hymns
were muttered quietly and as
we filed out I could hold back
no more as my eyes gave way
to tears as I walked away into
a day that needed drowning
in sorrow and alcohol.

THE NOSE JOB

'The bone structure of your nose
is completely abnormal, have you
experienced a facial injury?' the
ENT doctor asked:
'As a young man, I was involved
in countless physical altercations
with guys who seemed to hate
my nose, they'd punch it, kick it,
pulled and twisted it, spat at it
and shouted abuse at it, they
hated my nose' I replied;
'I see' she said concealing a
grin:
'I don't get involved in those
scenes nowadays' I said
reassuringly:
'That's good' she said
unimpressed
'Chances are you've treated
some of my opponents' I
said smiling: she didn't
respond as she tapped on a
keyboard:
'Goodbye Mr. Robinson, the results
will be sent to you' she said without
looking away from the screen.

ALL KINDS OF SHIT

'**M**other will lose it! We've got
to tell her about it in a public
place' she said
'Like a bar' I said
'Yes' she said
arrangements were made and
we were sat around a table in
a local pub:
'I'm pregnant' she told her
mother:
I looked out of the window
and held my girl's hand beneath
the table:
'You'll have to get rid of it
and he'll have to pay for it, a
private clinic, there is no more
to be discussed, get rid of it'
said her mother coldly,
rising from her seat and
walking away:
I sold guitars and amplifiers
and rare collectors records and
all kinds of shit:
I visited my girl in the
private clinic, it was a sad place,
full of sad, frightened and
ashamed young women:
several months later she
fucked-off to university
and I continued my pursuit
of drunkard.

THE LONESOME DRINK

For a couple of decades or more I
was a barfly:
I drank in bars all over town
morning, noon and night:
I saw gestures of drunken
kindness and sentiment and
acts of alcoholic violence
ignited by the most trivial
of matters, on occasions I
was involved in these
scenes of intoxicated
compassion or aggression,
I went with it, it's
what happened but I
never understood it or
even wanted to, it was a
world I inhabited for a
while, then I moved to
drinking in the streets
with the helpless, homeless,
deranged and beautiful
unpredictable alcoholics
and it was even uglier
than the bars and after a
few years I decided to
drink alone.

OVER THE WEEKEND

Read some short fiction by the
very eloquent, talented Kevin Tosca,
read some knock-out poems by the
legendary Cat McDaris,
took a stroll to buy some wine,
rolled joints and swallowed
some pills, watched a game of
soccer and my woman looks
fucking fantastic in a pair
of black thongs as she
simultaneously pleases us both
as the morning sun charges
and the sound of lawnmowers
crushes the birdsongs and the
hush of a hot July day,
I napped in the afternoon
and dreamt of freezing to
death: I sent out some poetry
submissions and fed my cats
numerous times and watched
the 1922 silent Nosferatu, I've
poured wine, thought of life,
yours and mine, thought of
death, yours and mine and
decided I could do nothing
about it, I listened to
classical music whilst I
emailed an editor in Athens,
then I switched off the
machine, it was dark outside
and I knew it was time
to let it go awhile.

FLEETING

She loved me just the one time,
I'll love her forever,
no doubt, she'd rightfully
forgotten about me by the
next day:
I was half-her age and she
should have known better,
but I'm thankful she didn't
and I loved her for it,
for the moments of
intensity and the surging
young macho imagination
of which she was
completely aware of and
accepted this ignorance
and my obvious flaws
and I loved her for it,
even today,
she did love me, albeit,
very briefly, she probably
can't remember and
cast the fleeting feelings
aside a long time ago
but that hot exchange
is here, now, alive
a world away from
where she is now.

THE COMMONPLACE

No more reaction than a
blink of an eye, like
something that is
commonplace, something
that doesn't count for
too much, like, it's
no surprise it's
happening again,
like a buzzing bee or
a crawling ant or a
drop of rain, it's all
the same, seen it before,
it's all too familiar,
routine.
that's how it felt when I
told her of my
forthcoming chapbook
and I knew it was useless
to try and explain how god
damn fortunate I am
for this to be happening,
how blessed and excited
I feel, so I didn't bother,
I kept my mouth shut as I
filled my glass in a
lonesome celebration.

PROTECTION

The jury heard how the 34-year-old
married man had filmed himself
sexually abusing and raping his
1-year-old daughter as she cried
and screamed in agony: he then
loaded the video onto a 'dark-
web' site and asked if any fucked-
up assholes had any suggestions
on how he could further viciously
violate his own baby:
he was sentenced to a minimum
of 70 years: in solitary
confinement for his own
protection:
all life is precious, yes,
but like everything else, there
are the exceptions where
that wonder and beauty and
compassion of life is not present
but is consumed by a vileness
of unspeakable, inhumane and
unimaginable abhorrent evilness:
particular animals, birds, fish,
insects, trees, lakes, oceans, forests
and lands are protected and their loss
would be an incalculable loss to the
planet:
he'll be in solitary confinement
for 70 years
for his own safety and protection
from the rest of the world:
there are a small number of

states in the USA where either
physical or medical castration
can be enforced following such
heinous sex crimes, unfortunately,
this fuck isn't resident in any
of those states.

IN THE FIRST FEW WEEKS

'The best part of you ran down
your mama's legs!' he screamed
just inches from my face;
'Yes, corporal! but at least I
knew my father' I foolishly
replied:
I could see the intensity of
anger raging in his eyes and
he backed away to prevent
himself from punching my
lights-out, after a few moments
a smile burnt into his face
and I knew I was in some
deep-shit here:
'Okay private, for the next
week I am making you,
personally, completely
responsible for the
cleanliness and tidiness of
your barracks, including
the shitters and bathrooms
and the floors, walls and
ceilings throughout, do
you understand private?'
'Yes Corporal' I wisely replied:
'If you fail in this duty, the
punishments will increase'
he said smiling:
I wondered what the fuck I
was doing here and things
didn't get any better.

THE PLANS

I wasn't a planned-for baby,
I was an accident,
unintentional,
nothing uncommon:
both of my parents were
born illegitimate and
never knew their father's:
I barely knew my father,
they divorced when I was 12,
nothing uncommon:
I've worked all my adult
life, fell in love, married,
have a daughter and 3
grandchildren: we have
brought houses, cars,
holidays:
nothing uncommon:
I am an alcoholic and
drug addict, I write poetry
and have had books
published,
 I am a publisher:
not so uncommon:
someday I'll die and
be forgotten
and that's common.

THE SUPERGLUE

The night before the poetry reading,
drunk, I sat on and busted my
spectacles but forgot all about it
until a few hours before the
reading the next day:
I was shot to pieces, earlier, I
unexpectedly came upon some
cash and purchased some
knock-out expensive hash along
with the codeine and diazepam:
I superglued the specs back-
together, smearing the lens,
making a right fucking mess:
some local newspaper
journalists were present to
cover the event, took
photographs and asked the
usual questions amongst the
small but warm crowd
but I was stoned and it
was a breeze and I sold a
couple of books and I left
quickly first chance I got
to go home and to pour a
glass of wine and forget all
about this
horrible business.

THE TOPLESS POEM

Topless, she moved gently
from side to side,
her breasts swaying with
the motion:
'Do you like them?'
she asked:
'I love them' I said
she cupped her tits and
asked again whether I
liked them: 'But they've
lost their shape!' she said
looking serious:
'Bullshit!' I said and
lunged forward:
she backed away
laughing, 'Let's not
get excited' she said
'Too late' I said as I
pushed open the
bedroom door, both of
us spontaneously
charged with an urge of
physical intimacy.

THE NUNCHUCK POEM

Out of curiosity, I purchased a
pair of training nunchucks,
thankfully made of foam
rather than wood: I would
have knocked myself
unconscious on numerous
occasions and inflicted
injuries and fractures to
my head, elbows, shoulders
and would have caused
damage to my
surroundings this past
month or so:
very surprisingly I am
becoming comfortable
and fluent with the basic
movements at a reasonable
speed, delivered directly
with least amount of effort
but striking with
maximum impact,
honest controlled and
precise, hitting the
imaginary opponent with
clarity,
hopefully,
the same movements I
make with my pen.

THE BABY CLOTHES

The 9 months pregnant married
teenager was initially lured to
the house with the promise of
free-baby-clothes: she was
welcomed by a mother in her
40's and her 2o-year-old
daughter:
as the mom distracted the
young mum, her daughter crept
up from behind and strangled her
with some electrical wire flex and
then the mother, savagely,
brutally, with a kitchen-knife,
cut the baby out of the corpse
and then she phoned the
emergency services;
the baby was brain-dead and
put on life-support:
the paramedics, surgeons,
nurses all assumed that the
40 year old was the mother
due to the blood upon her
clothing;
when the husband of his
young pregnant wife was reported
missing, the truth began
to emerge and the two
murderers were arrested:
the human intellect is both
beautiful and damned,
to plan and meditate such
horror is way beyond the

extreme of flawed senses:
the baby remains on life-
support
and his father lives on
in the darkness of the
world he no longer
cares for.

A 3 LEGGED DOG STORY

She was barely 15 years old and she
was frightened, petrified and couldn't
speaks to anyone,
she would shame herself
her family
and friends
and her village:
she must have felt overwhelming
desperation, trauma, guilt and
confusion like an avalanche of
certain suffering to come:
alone, she gave birth in a field
and buried the baby in a very
shallow grave and then walked
away: just a short while later
a 3 legged dog discovered the
baby during a walk with its
owner: the emergency
services were called and the
baby boy was taken into
hospital and was found
to be healthy:
several days later the mother
was arrested for attempted
murder;
her parents were outraged and
made no public comment and
hid away from their neighbours:
barely 15 years old
in lock-down in a psychiatric
hospital as she thinks of
her son, maybe, of her love for

him knowing she will never
see him as she awaits her
fate that will be decided by
a bunch of city educated
strangers.

She'd done it before, no doubt,
but always alone:
I asked her to do it for me
and I watched on as she did
and it was beautiful and
gentle, her delicate
fingers caressing and
pleasing: her eyes closed
and she leaned back with
a deep gasp and after a few
moments she looked at me
and could see that I was
ready to enter her
warm moistness as
Miles Davis'
'Blue in Green' seeped
from the radio.`

THE BABYSITTER

Some nights I'd be awoken
by her lovemaking with some
stranger she'd brought back
or she'd return alone and I'd
hear her pleasuring herself
with a buzzing vibrator as I
lay in darkness on the lounge
sofa as her toddler son
lay asleep in the next
room:
I was 14 years old and the
sounds were arousing,
surging and stimulating,
exciting and when it went
quiet, I'd have trouble
sleeping and in the
morning she'd make tea
and toast and occasionally
introduce me to the
pick-up asshole and
then she'd put some
money in my hand, kiss
me on the cheek and
thank me.

THE DOOR, THE DOG, THE DRAG

The unexpected, unwanted,
irritating knock at the door
always comes at the wrong
time because there isn't a
right time:
I opened up the door
slightly, keeping the barking
dog away with a foot:
a young 20 something suited
guy stood smiling dumbly,
holding a clutch of shiny
pamphlets:
'No' I said
'I'll call back later' he said
'Don't!' I said
'You're not interested?'
he asked
'No' I said
'You're not interested in
saving money?' he said
'No, I'm not interested
in saving money' I said
and closed the door:
fuck man, I'm not
interested in saving money,
more making and
spending the
fucking stuff.

THE SHOP-DOORWAY POET

He used to appear in town once a year,
for a week or so, dressed in rags,
filthy, shoes falling away from his
feet, sleeping in shop-doorways:
he had a beautiful toothless
smile that hid behind a scruffy
unkempt beard and he'd turn
up at poetry readings and get up
on stage and recite his scrambling
thoughts and the audience was
warm and friendly and he'd
anticipate free-drinks and was
usually obliged: he'd get drunk
and tell of outrageous stories
of his travels and of the
people along the way and he
was mesmerising:
I no longer read publicly
and haven't seen him for a
decade or so: I think of him
now as the cold rain falls
into the embrace of an ever
darkening night.

I MIGHT HAVE

I may have drank diablo under the table,
I may have been crucified before Christ
but for different reasons,
I may have written words that are
handcuffed to the gates of a child's
imagination and I may have
surrendered beautifully to the life
of a falling leaf,
of being engulfed in a fast rain
that journey's to where the world
is humbled by its own failure.

THE BUDGIES

'**M**y two budgies died within a week of each other,
the vet said the second bird died of a broken heart'
she said seriously, looking for a reaction:
'I'm really sorry to hear that, I'm sorry for your
loss and just a few hours ago 73 innocent people,
including women and children and the
elderly were massacred in the middle-east by
suicide bomb attacks' I said seriously, looking
for a reaction:
'Oh' she said, fluttering her eyes 'I need to
get to the supermarket, take care'. and she
walked away and so did I as the world does,
as its always done: it's all about loss, great
and small, measured by human sentiment
according to their present circumstances
but every loss belongs to us all.

After the climax,
a sense of satisfaction
and then, for a while,
lay back and submerge
into its wonder and the
inner rare warmth of
such experiences and
then where does one go?
to look for new
connections,
to give yourself freely
at the mercy of
strangers,
as always, to provoke
and tempt others to
commit to making the
work alive in books,
online publications and
zines and broadsides,
to push it forward in
hope of reaching
another climax.

SHE ANSWERED BEFORE I ASKED

'**W**hat is there for people like us?
I mean working-class-survival
people: where can we go except
the factories and warehouses and
shitty care-work, all lowly paid,
barely enough to keep alive
but with the unskilled,
unambitious, under-educated
workforce, the country would
fucking collapse,
what is there for you and I?
what do we want?
money is mostly the answer
and it's also the question:
cash dictates the quality of
living and without it you're
fucked, trapped in a shitty
laborious job, but its regular
and I can pay my rip-off
landlord rent and
often I wonder what the fuck
it's all for and all that
energy and uselessness
to survive and breed
more of the same.'

I'D LIKE TO KNOW

Just before and only just before
the deal goes down and the
hand-shakes have been
exchanged, just before
the sands let go the final
grain and the holy
signature has been spilt
across the age,
just before the song fades
and the candle flame
withers,
just before all of this that
was proceeded by the
decades of love and
madness,
just before the last
whispered breath of
poesy has been put to
sleep,
I'd like to know,
who'll pour wine
upon my grave.

John D Robinson is a UK poet.Hundreds of his poems have appeared online and in print. He has published numerous chapbooks and collections of his poetry. John was also nominated for a 2019/2020 Pushcart Prize, and is the Editor and Publisher behind the notorious *Holy&Intoxicated Publications*.

Publications:

When You Hear The Bell, There's Nowhere To Hide
Holy&Intoxicated Publications (UK) 2016 sold out

Cowboy Hats & Railways
Scars Publications (USA) 2016

An Outlaw In The Making
Scars Publications (USA) 2017

Hitting Home
Iron Lung Press (USA) 2018 sold out

The Pursuit Of Shadows
Analog Submission Press (UK) 2018 sold out

Too Many Drinks Ago
Paper and Ink Press (UK) 2018 sold out

Echoes Of Diablo
Concrete Meat Press (UK) 2018 sold out

Pushing Away The Hours
Alien Buddha Press (USA) 2018

Hang In There
Uncollected Press (USA) 2019

Singing Aria's
Analog Submission Press (UK) 2019 sold out

A Hash Smoking, Codeine Swallowing, Wine Drinking Son Of A Bitch
Alien Buddha Press (USA) 2019

The Sounds Of Samsara
Cyberwit Publishing (India) February 2020

Also Forthcoming in 2020:

3 Poets Series
East London Press (UK) March 2020

Red Dance
Uncollected Press (USA) March/April 2020

Smoking Herb and other Stories
Analog Submission Press (UK) April 2020

Also Available From
Cajun Mutt Press

Owls in Hot Rods with Pink Elephants and Dead Bats
by James D. Casey IV
ISBN# 1548246220

Haight
by Red Focks
ISBN# 172647125X

Absurd
by R. Bremner
ISBN# 1725983613

Isomorphic
by James D. Casey IV
ISBN# 1724001140

Dark Linings
by Joanne Olivieri
ISBN# 1727550374

Death & Love/Love & Death
by James D. Casey IV
ISBN# 1727853857

Juggernaut Fuzz
by Ryan Quinn Flanagan
ISBN# 1730783333

Also Available From
Cajun Mutt Press

This Many Years After The War
by Matthew Borczon
ISBN# 1731194226

Wild Rose Country
by R. Keith
ISBN# 0578439816

Detritus Of The Drunken Night
by Ian Lewis Copestick
ISBN# 1092511148

Dreams Of Mongolia
by Will Mayo
ISBN# 1093504102

Requiem for a Robot Dog
by Lauren Scharhag
ISBN# 1099369037

Unwritten Words That Slide Down The Wall
by James D. Casey IV
ISBN# 1099516676

Around the bend
By R. Keith
ISBN# 1696088925

Also Available From
Cajun Mutt Press

Miles of Sky Above Us, Miles of Earth Below
by Steve Denehan
ISBN# 057855996X

Stick Figure Opera
by Howie Good
ISBN# 1702328791

Hoodoo Voodoo
by Will Mayo
ISBN# 1711010421

Safer Behind Popcorn
by Sean Hanrahan
ISBN# 1652008691

Fracture Point
by Rani Whitehead
ISBN# 0578632861

Printed in Great Britain
by Amazon

36088020R00061